In Session:
A Collection of Healing Poems
by Valerie Domenech

Published by Sacred Journey Ministry

East Islip, NY 11730

www.overweightanxiousanddone.com

Copyright © 2023 Valerie Domenech

All rights reserved. No portion of this book may be reproduced in any form without permission from the publisher, except as permitted by U.S. copyright law. For permissions contact: valeriedomenech@gmail.com.

Cover by Valerie Domenech

ISBN: 979-8-9867141-7-2

The Practitioner reserves all rights. This book does not replace the advice of a medical professional. Please seek advice from the appropriate healthcare professional regarding any concerns, diagnoses, or treatments, as this book does not make any claims to diagnose, treat, or cure any physical, mental, emotional, or psychological ailments or conditions.

Disclaimer:

Valerie is a Holistic Minister Practitioner. Her ministry is Sacred Journey Ministry. As such, the following disclaimer applies:

PRIVATE LICENSE, INFORMED CONSENT, AND RELEASE:

*The undersigned hereby grants a Private License to the Minister Practitioner to provide/offer spiritual, mental, emotional, or intellectual materials and products to the undersigned.

The undersigned acknowledges that the Practitioner does not diagnose or prescribe for medical or psychological conditions nor claim to prevent, mitigate, or cure such conditions. The Practitioner does not provide diagnosis, care, treatment, or rehabilitation of individuals, nor does the Practitioner apply medical, mental health, or human development principles, but ministers to the suffering by prayer, spiritual, religious, or mental means.

The undersigned gives Informed Consent to the services that will be provided or materials/products that will be purchased. The undersigned hereby releases the Practitioner (and Church and all its local units, auxiliaries, affiliated organizations, ministers and agents) from all claims and liabilities arising from the use or misuse of spiritual, mental, emotional, or intellectual materials and products indemnifying and holding the Practitioner harmless from all claims and liabilities there from, whatsoever.

About the Author

As a secondary English teacher for the past twenty years, Valerie enjoys reading, but her true passion has always been writing. She has been able to use her love for writing as a means of healing. Valerie was officially diagnosed with multiple anxiety disorders over nineteen years ago and continues to work on her journey towards recovery. In addition to reading and writing and spending time with her son, Valerie enjoys being in nature, helping those in need, and spreading kindness.

Thank you for purchasing this book!

With gratitude,

Valerie

Introduction

Writing poetry has been a cathartic and therapeutic experience for me. Ever since I was fourteen-years old, I have been writing poetry as a means of self-expression and release. Today, I notice the difference in my anxiety levels and how I feel when I write compared to when I don't write. It makes a difference.

Some may read my poems and recall specific experiences a little differently than I do. It's important to remember that everyone's perception and understanding are different. The way different people remember the same event may also vary. Therefore, my recollection of certain events is *my* truth, *my* interpretation of different events that transpired in my life. Perhaps others' truths may be different or they might recall events differently. That's okay. The beautiful thing about that is that none of us is wrong. In fact, all of our perspectives are right.

It is my hope that you will see my process of recovery through my poetry, as expressing myself in this genre has truly been instrumental on my journey to inner peace, happiness, and fulfillment.

Table of Contents

Panic Attack..6
Summer Barbecue...8
Coward...10
Fat Girl...14
Fabricated Reality...16
Mother's Day..18
Well-Intentioned...21
This Is Trauma..24
Keeping It Real...27
This Poem..29
Without My Anxiety..32
Mental Illness...36
Flirt..41
Notice Me...44
Teeter-Tottering..47
Little Girl..50

Panic Attack

With two fingers over my carotid artery,
I begin to count.
1. 2. 3. 4. 5. 6. 7. 8. 9. 10...
100 heartbeats per minute.

I hold two fingers to my neck and count again.
1.2.3.4.5...

My left ear vibrates with each pulsation.
The shallow breaths make my chest rise and fall
like an Olympian's after the 50km race.

I prod and poke at my sternum
until the bruises and soreness finally indicate
a life-threatening condition.

It is then I imagine my heart stopping
and envision the future without me.

My child, mourning his mother.
My husband, slightly relieved.
My mother, completely broken.

I count yet again.
1, 2, 3, 4, 5...

I cannot lift the armor
that confines my chest.
I know I must stand up.

I must move, breathe, distract.

Yet, I remain seated
with two fingers covering
the soft hollow in my neck,
wondering if my heart just skipped a beat
as I begin to count again.

Summer Barbecue

I wondered if anyone would notice
that I was wearing jeans
and a three-quarter sleeve shirt
instead of a bathing suit and shorts.

I wondered if anyone would notice
that I was scoping out the seating
looking for a chair that wouldn't collapse under me.

I wondered if the swing chair would snap
or the wooden bench would crack
or if my ass would hit the ground if I planted it
on that hammock.

I wondered if the arms of that teak chair
would dig into my hips,
if my fat would spill off the sides,
or if I'd be able to wiggle my way out
when it was time to get up.

I wondered if they would notice
that I brought a fresh garden salad
and if they would joke that I should try eating that sometime
instead of doughnuts and cake.

I wondered if anyone would talk to me
or if they wouldn't want to be seen with the fat girl,
you know, the girl who's wearing jeans
in the middle of August.

I watched all the women in bikinis
daintily sipping fruity cocktails
and wondered if they would notice
all my stomach rolls hiding under my oversized shirt.

I watched as they all enjoyed the barbecue
and I longed for cooler weather where I wouldn't look
so out of place in clothing that did not reveal any bare skin.

I watched as they ate freely
adding a mix of foods to their plates
as I snacked on celery and carrot snacks
acting as though that were my regular fare.

I fooled them, I thought,
as I wondered if they even noticed me at all.

Coward

How much pain she must have been in
to end her life the way she did.
Some say she was a coward
who took the easy way out.
How selfish she was to only think of herself
and not her family and friends whom she left behind.
The pain   caused *them*,
the hurt *she* created,
the memories they would have to cling to
to remember her, to hear her voice.
How selfish, how cowardly, just spineless
to take her own life like that,
to try to numb the pain with all of those pills and patches.
How egotistical.
Self-serving.
Opportunistic even.

How selfish to try to escape from her pain,
to suffer in silence in a room filled with others.
To book a motel room,
take with her only prescription bottles,
and leave before anyone else was even awake.
How arrogant
to write letter after letter
to loved ones she would leave behind
telling them what they meant to her,
so they would have that remembrance from her
for as long as they chose to hold onto it.
How self-serving.

To weep, alone, in a dingy motel room,
for which she paid cash
so as to have the last day of her life to herself,
without trace,
no credit card,
no cell phone,
no notice.
To know she was heading to her death
alone
in a strange place.
What a coward.

You didn't think about them
all happy, living their lives
enjoying weekend getaways,
happy hours, and get-togethers.
You didn't think how this would affect them,
even though they hadn't called,
hadn't invited you to dinner,
to go away
to get together.
How dare you.

How much pain you must have been in
to end your life the way you did.
Alone, in a dingy motel room,
with vials of prescription pills in your stomach
and pain-numbing patches stuck all over your body.
What a thoughtless, inconsiderate deed.

I wasn't invited to their last happy hour,

or on their girls' weekend,
or to our regular monthly dinner at our favorite local
restaurant.

I didn't get a phone call or a text
or a quick unannounced visit just to check in.
How much pain I was in as I suffered
alone, at home, in the darkness
without a friend, an invite, a call, a text.
Never a thought in their minds that I might need someone.

I selfishly sat home alone not reaching out.
I arrogantly did not check in
or send a text
or invite myself over.
Too self-absorbed to make plans with others;
Too self-serving to make a phone call.

How much pain I was in
as I walked over to the medicine cabinet
and contemplated taking the easy way out.
Contemplated running off,
alone
to a dingy, unknown place.
No trace, no records, no contact.
To write letter after letter to those left behind
as I swallow pill after pill,
handful after handful,
and lie down
on a dirty, unwashed comforter
as I wait for the pain to finally cease.

How selfish I am.
How cowardly.

Fat Girl

It kills me to hear you make fun of fat people like that.
I'm like, *Hello, I'm right here. Don't you see me?*
I mean, it's kinda hard to miss me.
What am I supposed to do
when you mock that fat pig over there?
Am I supposed to agree with you?
Laugh with you?
Am I right? Do you see her? I'm right, right?
No there's nothing right with you,
nothing right about you.
Nothing at all.

She's so disgusting.
How does she look at herself in the mirror every day?
Why is she even alive right now?
Keep stuffing your face, fatty!

How many times do I have to listen to you?
What a whale.
She's so big.
Damn, her layers flow over the edge of that chair.
She's gross.
Fat people smell.
Oh look how she almost fell
off that chair that's too small for her.
Don't seat her next to me;
I need some room to breathe.

She has such a pretty face.

If only she lost weight.
What a shame.
Do you think her parents are to blame?
If only she could exhibit some self-control.
Oh sweetheart, please put down that buttered roll.

There are days I don't want to be here,
listening to you ridicule me and mock me
with every chance you get.
Your words taunt me, haunt me, flaunt your indecency.

But here I am,
fat, loud, and in your face.
Move over because I'm coming to invade your space.
See that empty seat right next to you?
Well, clear the way
because I'm coming through.

Fabricated Reality

I have to stop,
stop doing this to myself.
Stop fearing, and worrying, and panicking
that the seemingly inevitable is going to happen
and that the world as I know it is going to end.

I say it every time,
that even though I have convinced myself in my mind
that the worst will happen,
I know that will not be the end result.
It never is.

I create stories in my head,
fearing the worst, creating dread.
The worst case scenario is definitely up ahead.
Even though the opposite will be true instead,
I still continue to craft tales.

Tales of fiction that I fear will turn
into my reality and I won't be able to discern
fantasy narratives that fabricate my reality
from nonfiction accounts that form this duality.

Only, there's nothing real about this version
but fear.
Every time I make myself sick
over the possibility of the worst,
my pain and suffering is always in vain.

know this to be true,
even as my limbs go numb and my body starts to tingle,
that my worst fears only serve to rekindle
the trauma I lived as a child.

Yet, as much awareness and knowledge as I have,
it doesn't stop the avalanche of worry that falls overhead.
Instead, I just look at the snow
that continues to rapidly flow
down the mountainside under which I stand
just watching it fall and take command.

And as I stand underneath and it covers me all,
I know I just have to remember and recall
that I can choose to step aside whenever I want,
as I continue to stand, frozen,
as the snow covers me all.

Mother's Day

You brought my favorite desserts over for Mother's Day,
cannolis with and without chocolate chips,
assorted miniature pastry, and strawberry cheesecake.
I should be thanking you for your kindness,
for thinking about me on my special day,
but instead I'm wishing you away,
wishing you didn't stay,
wishing you realized how you did betray
me.

You brought me my favorite desserts on Mother's Day,
as a way to celebrate,
and you didn't hesitate,
and said it was to dedicate
the day to me.

But when you brought me my favorite desserts on Mother's Day,
it felt like you brought me a bottle
when I was only 45 days sober.

It felt like you brought me some blow
when I was just 45 days clean.

It felt like you wanted me to succumb to my addiction
because you wanted me to feel good
even if feeling good could eventually kill me.
Because that's the only way you ever knew how to console me.

It felt like you didn't care.
It felt like you wanted to see me to fail,
give into temptation so I could be derailed,
lose control so my arms and legs flail.

It felt like you disagreed
like you didn't want me to succeed,
so instead you continue to try to overfeed
me.

But you're the one who failed because instead of surrendering to the binge,
I wasn't even tempted.

Because your fancy Italian pastries only reminded me
that this is not about you anymore.

I'm not that fragile, dependent little child
who you used to shut up with a Happy Meal from McDonald's.

I am the epitome of strength, a fighter,
who won't be led by you to the slaughter.
In fact, I am everything you are not,
not defined by being your daughter.

Your attempt to sabotage me only succeeded in strengthening me,
in making me even more dedicated to overcoming this binge
eating and the patterns from my infancy.

You see, when you brought me my favorite desserts on
Mother's Day,

you affirmed what I knew deep down inside.
I don't need food to comfort me.
You lied.

Well-Intentioned

I know you meant well when you told me
God was calling me to him,
when you said only God could stop my panic attacks
and that Jesus was waiting for me with open arms.
I know you meant well.

But sometimes what we mean
doesn't exactly translate that way
because what I heard was something very different
from what you may have intended.

When you spoke those words so seemingly good-intentioned,
I heard you calling me a pagan.
I heard you imply that my suffering was a result
of my lack of your version of Christian worship.

What I heard is that you assume
that I don't believe in Jesus
and that I have to believe in him the way you believe in him.
You assumed that I don't have God in my life
or that I'm even interested in your interpretation of religion
or how you believe it can help me.
Don't assume that I am or that I do,
but also don't assume that I do not.
How about you just don't assume?

Would you be offended if I tried to convert you,
tried to tell you what to believe simply because I believe it to be true?

Did I even ask you who you know?
Would you be open to listening to me tell you your
suffering is due to the way you pray?

What if your beliefs didn't align with mine?
More importantly, what if they already did and you've isolated me,
denied me because you've misjudged me?

You assume that it's okay to tell me what I need and how I need it,
that my relationship with *him* has to replicate *yours*
else I will suffer eternal damnation and panic attacks for the rest of my life.
Your ego is showing.

What I heard is that you know God better than I do,
that your relationship with him, or her, or it
is stronger than mine,
that mine is wrong and yours is right.

What I heard you say is that your version of truth is absolute as you
continue to dispute and refute
in your goal to recruit
me.

What I heard is you assume, accuse, and in turn abuse
all in your attempt to spread the Good News.

I think you meant well when you told me
God was calling me to him,
that Jesus was waiting for me with open arms
to stop my panic attacks and rid me of my anxiety.

I think you meant well.

Although perhaps opposite from what you intended,
your words only succeeded in insulting and offending.
Dripping with arrogance and superiority,
it's people like you who are the source of my anxiety.

This Is Trauma

Keep your pity to yourself.
There's no room for it here.
I know what this is.

This is trauma,
trauma from being told
at five years old
that I was the reason for my mother's kidney infection.
Since I was such a bad girl,
Mommy had to stay in the hospital
and she might not come back
if I don't get my act
together.

Because I didn't listen,
while mommy was cooking in the kitchen,
she wanted to get away from me,
to see what life was like without a rotten child like me.

This is trauma,
trauma from being told
at 10 years old
that I was the reason for their divorce.
I made Mommy and Daddy fight during the night
when I would try to climb into their bed.
And because of that,
Daddy was leaving.

Because I didn't listen

when Daddy gave his instructions
to go back to my room
and sleep by myself,
like a big girl, but instead a bad girl.

This is trauma,
trauma from being told
at fifteen years old
that my stepdad beat my mother
because I made things difficult.
If I weren't there, they would still be together.
No black eyes, no broken noses,
no beatings for good measure.

Because I was an instigator
a spoiled brat, a trouble maker.
It was my fault he hit her.
It was my fault he left her.
It was my fault things fell apart.

This is trauma,
trauma from being told
at 16 years old
that I had to get a job.
That I needed to contribute to the household,
buy food, my own clothes,
work at McDonald's, I suppose.

Because I wanted too much.
Because I needed too much.
Because I was selfish and spoiled much.

This is trauma,
trauma from being told
at 20 years old
that I was simply not marriage material,
not the kind of girl you'd bring home to mother.

Because I was too promiscuous,
I was just good enough for a post drunken rush.
Not to be taken out to dinner
or god forbid to be seen in public.
Only good enough to get you off quick.

This is trauma,
trauma from being told
at 46 years old
that I never was and never will be good enough.

Because I am not smart enough.
Because I am not thin enough.
Because I am not interesting enough.
Because I am not important enough.

Because I am too...
me.

Because what it comes down to is:

This is trauma,
trauma from all I've been told
since I was just five years old.

Keeping It Real

Like a chameleon
you change who you are
based on who you're with at the moment.

Masked by versatility and flexibility,
you pretend to be someone you're not
trying to fit in
desperately trying to find your place,
your space,
in this world.

Do you even know who you are?
What you really like, what you really don't?

A chameleon who changes color
to be liked, to be accepted.
To fit in, not for protection.
Opportunist. Conformist.
Fake.

Unlike you, I don't try to fit in.
Lose myself, play myself, tell myself I need to be
someone I'm not just to do the things I'd rather not.

I'm logical like that,
constant like that
authentic like that.
Real.

You say I'm basic
because I listen to Miley Cyrus and Justin Bieber
and maybe I do blast
the whole Dirty Dancing album in my car.
No I'm not into rock, heavy metal, or grunge.
It's just not my idea of fun.

I know who I am.

I set boundaries,
stay home when I'm tired,
wanting to hang out
but refusing to sacrifice myself in the process.
Anything but basic,
although it's hard for you to face it.

And who do you think you are?
Trying to inflict pain and leave scars?
The only scars you're leaving behind
are the unhealed ones on your own heart.

You can tell me I'm cliché
as you try to keep up with the different personalities you portray.
But you can't rattle me, can't shatter me, can't batter me.

I know who I am.

So I'm gonna go now and listen to a little Despacito
and you could just go fuck yourself, un poquito.

This Poem

No, this poem is not about you.
You have to understand
I may use the things people say as inspiration,
but that doesn't mean my poems are about them.
About you.
It's called creative license.

I mean, this poem couldn't be about you
because then that might hurt your feelings.
It might make you feel bad for something you did
or something you said.
And I don't want you to feel bad.

I mean, if this poem was about you
then you might know how your words
made me feel
and how your actions have hurt me.
I mean, if this poem was about you
then you might get mad at me
for saying how I feel
for letting loose the great reveal
that you're a bully and a fucking heel.

If this poem was about you
you might try to get revenge.
But why would you do that if you were my friend?

If this poem was about you,
you might not like me anymore.

You might reject me, try to wreck me, try to inject me
with your shame and insecurity.

Of course this poem isn't about you.
I mean, if it was, you might exclude me,
you might mock me.
It might change the way you view me.

I can't write a poem about you.
I don't want to be mocked, or ridiculed
or be called names or be abused.

Or can I?
Can I write a poem about how I always try to please
and you in turn try to squeeze and seize until I heave?
Yet, now I foresee
someone being held accountable for who she is.

I'm writing a poem about me,
how I want you to let me be me,
to let me be free,
so I can be the me you're afraid for me to be.

This poem is about me,
fighting for my life, my sense of self
fighting against you and your fabricated self.

I don't care anymore what you think of me,
Don't even feel guilty if you're offended by my poetry.
Maybe next time you should mind your tongue
if you're afraid of being hung

out to dry in front of all of these inquiring eyes.

No, this poem is not about you.
Oh, fuck it.
Of course this poem is about you.
It always fucking was.

Without My Anxiety

I feel like I can't breathe,
like the weight of thousands of repressed memories
have me in a WWE chest lock.
As I try to inhale, my lungs don't expand.
Instead, they push against my diaphragm
attempting to get some air.
It feels like someone is doing CPR compressions
on my chest,
someone trying to keep me from breathing,
trying to hold me down,
even though I know that's the only thing keeping my brain
oxygenated.

It's like a mind fuck,
like the thing that is robbing me of life
is the only thing keeping me alive.
It's like the thing that destroys each and every day
is the only way I know how to survive.

Fuck this shit.

It's like I'm stuck on a hamster wheel
spinning and turning
and panting and gasping for air.
Looking back
wondering if it's going to get me
going to trip me
going to make me fall.
But I keep getting back on

just to keep running
in place.

It's like a drug that calls my name
releasing dopamine in my brain.
It's like impossible to avoid
this healthy mind being destroyed.

It's like someone squeezing my stomach from the inside
making tears flow from my eyes.
I want it to stop.
I beg it to stop.
I plead with the universe to make it go away,
only to summon it back by the end of the day.

I feel like I can't breathe,
as my chest starts to heave
and I make myself believe
that the anxiety is my enemy.

And even though I claim to want it to go away,
I clutch the fear and worry to my chest
and hold on for dear life.
For who would I be without my anxiety?

Who would I be without the panic,
the worry,
the fear?
What would I hear
in my mind if not my own intrusive thoughts
paralyzing me,

rendering me immobile physically and mentally?

I say I want it to go away,
that it causes too much pain,
but I think that maybe the anxiety
is a way for me to mask the pain.

As the pain starts to surface,
my protector begins to fulfill its purpose.
It's not the panic and worry I need to fear;
It's the feelings I feel
and the voices I hear
when anxiety isn't even near.

Who am I?
Who would I even be without my anxiety?
A scared little girl?
An insecure teen?
A broken young woman?
Or maybe just an aging robotic machine?

The thing I despise the most
is the thing that comforts me the most.
The thing I am running from
is the thing I keep running to.

It's not the anxiety crippling me.
It's the pain and trauma that plead for it to shield me
For who would I be without my anxiety?
A vulnerable little girl replaying painful memories
without anyone to protect me?

Quick! Where are you panic, fear, and worry?
I need you here to guard and distract me
from the trauma that lives in my every cell.
For without my anxiety,
I'm living in an even more tormenting hell.

Mental Illness

It's hard to understand how my mind works.
You see, I've been diagnosed
with Generalized Anxiety Disorder,
Panic Disorder,
Obsessive Compulsive Disorder,
Hypochondriasis,
and, consequently, Binge Eating Disorder.

I used to be afraid of admitting all that,
all those diagnoses,
out of fear people would think I'm crazy.
But I don't think that way anymore.
I mean, people might think I'm crazy with or without my slew of
mental disorders.
I just don't care what they think about them or me
because I'm standing in my truth,
speaking my truth in order to heal myself
and perhaps provide comfort and understanding to others.

You see, I'm here sharing my trauma, my pain, and my fears
so I no longer have to hide, no longer have to guise
who I am.
So you no longer have to hide
who you are.

It's not as if I like to label myself,
add myself to some psychology textbook category
so I can become that stereotype.
It's just that that "label" helps me understand,

helps me take command,
of what's going on in my head.

Persistent worrying,
overthinking everything,
fear of the unknown,
of change,
feeling like I'm always in danger.
I'm either running and taking flight
or arming myself for a fight.
I'm always tired, always nervous,
always edgy on the surface.
Why hasn't she texted me back?
Did she misread my tone?
Why did I try to be funny? (I'm not funny.)
Should I send another text?
Should I clarify what I meant?
And as if that weren't debilitating enough,
then the panic sets in and really makes it rough,
seemingly decorating my wrists like cuffs
holding me prisoner to myself.

I'm dying. I'm definitely dying. I can't breathe.
My heart is racing; it's about to give out.
I should go to the emergency room now,
so there's a chance they can save me.
I'm dizzy. I can't feel my legs. I'm going to black out.

You'd think I'd be able to recognize the symptoms by now
instead of giving into the fear and irrational thoughts.

But I can't.
Instead I refer to the obsessive thoughts and images in my head,
impossible to control, taking over what feels like my soul.

Unreasonable imaginings lead to compulsions that have me spiraling,
that lead me to recycling
these thoughts that have me dialing
911.

Until I hang up because what if this is just anxiety again?
It's not. I'm dying this time and if I don't call, this will be it.
But what if this is just a panic attack?
It's not. It feels different.
The pain is sharper, wider, stronger.

I continue to poke and prod as if with a stick
trying to awaken the beast
or find where it is sick.

Wondering if I should pick up the phone again
that is when
I decide it's then
time to Google my symptoms.
I know what I will find,
but I just need the mental relief of seeing it on the screen
just that one time.

Until I come across something that tells me
I am most definitely
having a cardiac event.

So I continue searching one site after another
that tells me I am in fact most likely dying,
until I reach the one that says it could be a panic attack
and I am relieved and my logic starts to come back.

Until the thoughts reappear
and I've already worried, panicked, Googled, and feared.

I turn to the next thing that brings me comfort
and that's what's in the fridge, the cabinets, and the cupboards.
I stuff my face until it's all gone.

That pain in my leg is a blood clot,
so I finish the bag of chips.
That headache is a brain tumor,
so I swallow the sleeve of cookies.

I am full and can't get another piece of food down,
but I am sick and I am dying,
so I am stuffing and trying
to make the sickness go away.

It's hard to understand how my mind works,
how the thoughts flow like a violent whitewater river
that can potentially flip my raft over
and leave me gasping,
leave me thrashing,
leave me flailing
with no life preserver in sight.
Who knows? It might not,

but what if it just might.
What if I'm sick?
What if I die?
It's not likely that that will happen,
What if, it's just anxiety?
Imagine?

Flirt

Constantly seeking external validation,
I fight the urge to trust myself.
Tell me I'm beautiful.
I look to men for comments on how young I look,
how blue my eyes are,
how sexy that color lipstick looks on my lips.
I eat up the attention
and feel good about being noticed,
being desired
being considered attractive,
by someone other than my husband,
by your husband.

I'm easy,
too easy,
to get to fall for him.
All he has to do
is just shoot me a glance,
hold the door open for me,
tell me my hair color
brings out the color in my eyes
and I'm his.

It's that easy to lure me,
that easy to secure me.
All he has to do is pretend to adore me.
It's that easy.

And I kind of feel bad

and I'm kind of sorry,
but not even the guilt
will make me stop.
Because every day I'm dying inside.
Every day I'm trying outside
not to let you see
that I am not doing okay.

Because every day I'm lonely
and I'm hurting, so I mask with pain with the flirting
and I'm getting tired of lying
about how I'm doing okay.

So I bat my eyes and feign interest in his stories,
give him attention so he would show me some affection,
as I show some cleavage in exchange for feeling loved.
If only for that short window of time
I feel wanted,
I feel desired,
I feel important.

Because in that moment
I don't care that I'm cheating,
that he's your husband,
that I'm just a unmemorable momentary physical release.

Because, even if just for that moment,
I can forget how I'm dying inside.
So I cover the pain on the outside,
as I mask the hurting with the flirting
to convince you that I am okay.

I am not okay.

Notice Me

I mask the pain with a smile,
with bright, purple lipstick
and globs of mascara
that the tears will end up washing away.

I smile through the pain
even though I feel like I want to die.
Even though I fear death,
I also fear life.
I smile to conceal the hurt
as I touch up my mascara
and wonder if you could even tell
I was crying.

I force myself to go out
and I sob the entire car ride
wishing I had stayed home
but knowing why I didn't.
Did you even notice?

My eyes don't look exactly right.
My makeup isn't as perfect.
I look a little disheveled
and something just seems off.
Did you notice?

I start to panic about something trivial,
something irrational,
that didn't even happen,

that wasn't even factual.
Did you notice?

I'm smiling and that's all you can see
I'm hiding so that I don't reveal
that I'm falling apart,
that I'm not who I appear to be.
Did you notice?

Did you notice that my voice cracked
just a little as we talked on the phone?
I cleared my throat so you wouldn't hear,
laughed awkwardly to guise the fear.
Did you hear it?

I apply layer upon layer
of black lash-intensifying mascara
to diminish the appearance of redness and swelling.
I add yet another coat
of long-wearing lip stain
to create another focal point,
a distraction,
so you wouldn't notice.
Did you notice?

Concealed behind a mask
of drug store cosmetics,
I applied more and more synthetics,
so that you will focus on the aesthetics
all in an attempt to distract and avoid,
to prevent you from seeing how I'm completely destroyed.

Did you notice?
Oh god, how I hope you noticed.

Teeter-Tottering

I'm teeter-tottering
between fearing my own death
and wishing I would die,
between the ups and downs
of the adrenaline of worrying
and the sluggishness of sadness.

My ups are not really ups.
They are momentary surges of energy
that consume my thoughts and guise my pain.
My downs are not really downs.
They are temporary intermissions
between moments of pure panic and intrusive thoughts.

But they pull, and they weigh,
and they seem to say
that none of this matters anyway.
The sadness sits on my chest
rendering my lungs able to take in
just enough air to keep me alive,
yet not enough to make me feel
like I will actually survive
this.

I'm teeter-tottering
between wanting to release the obsessions
and wanting to hold on,
between wanting to be free
from the constraints of my mind

and wanting to remain in the comfort of the discomfort.

The very thinking that holds me captive
also provides the safety of the familiar
creating a tug-of-war between
irrationality and reason,
sickness and health,
literal death or life.

I'm teeter-tottering
between loving myself
and hating myself,
between living in my truth
and trying to please others,
between liking myself
and wanting others to like me.
Between fearing a life of pain
and fearing a life of joy.
Between all the what ifs
and just being present.

I'm teeter-tottering,
but it's not a game.
There's no one at the other end.
I'm fluctuating and vacillating
yet the weight is one-sided
and even though it keeps me anchored
I am not stable.

And I wish I wasn't contemplating
and that my thoughts weren't manipulating

and that my mind wasn't indoctrinating
me into believing that I am less than.

I'm teeter-tottering
between up and down,
between laughter and tears,
as I rise and fall,
rise and fall,
between up and down,
between life and death.

I teeter-totter.

Little Girl

My chest is heavy
and I feel like I can't breathe.
Is it anxiety,
or am I having a heart attack?
Is it fear,
or do I need to go to the hospital?

After 19 years I still don't know
at first.
I worry that I'm dying,
but inside I know I'm not
yet.

But the pain in my chest
the heaviness on my breast
the shortness of breath
and the fear of death
overcome me and I can't move.

Do I give into it
and succumb to the shallow breaths?
Or do I try to fight it
and push back against the fear?

Am I dying?
No, not today.
But what if I am
and what if I do?
Will it really happen this time

or is it just my skewed point of view?
Again.

My shoulders begin to tighten
and my neck becomes sore.
I don't want to live like this anymore.

I know what is happening,
but I don't trust myself
to look past the physical manifestations of my trauma
and have the confidence to listen to what I know is true in my gut.

I'm not having a heart attack,
I finally say to myself.
You're safe,
even though you weren't then.
I say to the little girl inside me
nudging me to call an ambulance.

We are not okay, she cries.
She's not trying to scare me;
she truly believes we are both in danger.

I love you, I say to her,
but I will not let you get into the driver's seat.
I'm driving this car.
So sit in the back, put your seatbelt on, and enjoy the view.
Nothing is going to happen to you,
or me.
Even though you're scared of being hurt again,
you can finally trust

*that I got you
and the pain you went through
will finally be subdued.
You know that love and protection
you wanted as a child?
Well, I'm giving it to you now.*
With tears in her eyes and relief on her face
she offered a smile.

And just like that
the pain in my chest abates
the heaviness on my breast dissipates
the shortness of breath evaporates
and the fear of death disintegrates.
And suddenly I am at peace.

www.ingramcontent.com/pod-product-compliance
Lightning Source LLC
Chambersburg PA
CBHW061958070426
42450CB00011BA/3204